Sweetness

The Courage and Heart of
Walter Payton

TRIUMPH
BOOKS

CHICAGO

Contents

4   **A Remarkable Run**

Payton lived each of his forty-five years like a champion

20   **In a Class by Himself**

When push came to shove, nobody was better

30   **Sweet Memories: A Photo Gallery**

48   **Destiny Calls**

The '85 championship was the pinnacle of his career

62   **A Heart of Gold**

Payton's greatness was matched only by his generosity

66   **The Softer Side of Sweetness**

Off the field, he touched family, friends,
and teammates

74   **A Hero's Farewell**

Thousands gathered for a Soldier Field memorial

86   **Payton's Place: A Photo Gallery**

a Remarkable run

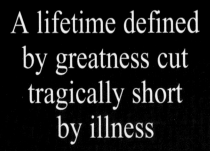

A lifetime defined by greatness cut tragically short by illness

By Tom Johnson and David Fantle

Sweetness. Seldom has a nickname better reflected the true measure of a man than this gentle description of legendary Hall-of-Fame running back Walter Payton. In a punishing game where victory can be measured in inches, Payton gained yards and broke records. His all-time rushing record of 16,726 yards still stands.

Against huge odds—especially early in his career when many Chicago Bears teams were perennial underdogs—Payton churned up the record yardage and almost single-handedly carried his team to flashes of respectability by the late '70s and then ultimately helped turn the franchise into a powerhouse during the mid-'80s.

So it came as a shock to just about everyone when Payton, perhaps the greatest all-around player in league history, succumbed to bile duct cancer on Nov. 1 at the age of 45. Payton died at noon at his suburban Chicago home with his wife Connie, son Jarrett and daughter Brittney at his bedside.

a Remarkable run

Payton set the standard for durability and productivity by a running back. Nobody ran with a football more times for more yards.

His toughest opponent

Although Payton had been battling the rare liver disease (officially termed primary sclerosing cholangitis) for more than a year, it seemed that an ironman who had beaten the odds for so long—missing just one game during his 13-year career—would somehow prevail against the ravaging disease.

The only treatment for Payton's liver disease was a transplant, but the onset of cancer precluded that option.

"A known complication of this liver disease is this type of cancer," said Dr. Greg Gores of the Mayo Clinic, where Payton received treatment after revealing his disease to the public last February. "Unfortunately, Walter's malignancy was very advanced and progressed very rapidly."

Payton was diagnosed with PSC in the fall of 1998 and revealed it at a press conference in February after he felt compelled to explain a dramatic weight loss. PSC is a rare disease in which the bile ducts inside and outside the liver narrow because of inflammation and scarring. This causes bile to accumulate in the liver and results in damage to liver cells. It's a progressive disease that leads to cirrhosis and liver failure. The exact cause of PSC is unknown.

Mike Singletary, a former teammate and fellow Hall of Famer, said he prayed and read Scriptures with Payton over the weekend.

"Outside of anything I've ever seen—the greatest runs, the greatest moves—what I experienced this weekend was by far the best by Walter Payton," said Singletary.

Former Bears head coach Mike Ditka called Payton "the greatest Bear of all," and Bears owner Virginia McCaskey paid special tribute to Payton. "After Brian Piccolo died (in 1970), my husband Ed and I promised ourselves we wouldn't be so personally involved with any of the players," she said tearfully. "We were able to follow that resolve until Walter Payton came into our lives."

One of a kind

In 13 seasons with the Bears from 1975-87, Payton set NFL records for total yardage (16,726) and rushing attempts (3,838), both of which still stand. His 10 seasons with more than 1,000 or more yards, his 275 yards in one game and his 77 games with more than 100 yards rushing also stand as all-time marks.

From the time he arrived in the city as a No. 1 draft choice from Jackson State in 1975, Payton's punishing running style and charismatic personality earned him the admiration of Chicagoans starved for sports heroes. For years, Payton carried a team with less talent until his efforts were rewarded with a Super Bowl ring in 1985.

Payton set the standard for durability and productivity by a running back, outlasting and outgaining all who went before. Marcus Allen later played in more games and scored more rushing touchdowns, but nobody ran with a football more times for more yards.

In a sport defined by runners from the time football's unwitting inventor picked up a soccer ball and ran with it, Payton outdid them all, leaving Jim Brown, O.J. Simpson, Tony Dorsett, Franco Harris, Eric Dickerson, John Riggins and the rest in his wake. In a city proud of its tradition of runners from

a Remarkable run

From the time he arrived as a No. 1 draft choice in 1975, Payton's punishing running style and charismatic personality earned the admiration of Chicagoans.

Red Grange to Bronco Nagurski to Gale Sayers, Payton outperformed them all.

Arguments over who was the greatest runner hinge on style and opinion. Simpson and Dorsett were faster. Jim Brown and many others were bigger. Sayers, some say, was more graceful. Earl Campbell, Larry Csonka and Nagurski may have been more powerful, although pound for pound, nobody was stronger than Payton.

Ditka, the Bears' coach for Payton's final six seasons, said that he was the best football player he had ever seen because he could do so many things so well. For example, Payton found time to catch more passes than either Lenny Moore or Frank Gifford, two running backs who became the first great flankers as the passing game developed.

Payton was such a superb blocker that coaches liked to save clips to show friends. "He's a thrill to watch for a football man," said Abe Gibron, who missed being Payton's first coach by a year. Those sentiments were echoed by coach Frank O'Connor, who said after first seeing Payton play, "God must have taken a chisel and said, 'I'm going to make me a halfback.'"

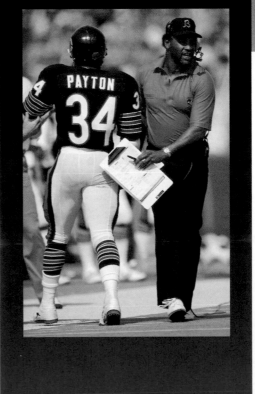

a **Remarkable** run

There are many opinions as to who was the greatest running back. Some were faster, and many were bigger. But pound for pound, nobody was stronger than Payton.

By the numbers

Walter Jerry Payton was born July 25, 1954 in Columbia, Miss. He didn't play football until the 11th grade at Columbia High School. He liked music and preferred the band to achievements on the gridiron (in college, he was even a finalist in the national "Soul Train" dance contest). But the first time he ever carried a football, he ran 60 yards for a touchdown. He never looked back.

After shedding the childhood nickname "Spiderman," Payton picked up "Sweetness" at Jackson State, a school he chose over larger schools because his brother, Eddie, played ball there. By the time he graduated from Jackson State in 1974, with a bachelor's degree in special educa-

---

On Oct. 7, 1984, Payton broke Brown's career rushing mark of 12,312 yards with a 6-yard run against the New Orleans Saints.

---

tion, he was the leading scorer in NCAA history. In three and a half years (Payton graduated early) he had racked up 65 touchdowns and rushed for 3,563 yards.

On Jan. 28, 1975, the Chicago Bears made Payton their first pick in the NFL draft (the 4th player overall), and the very next year he was voted to the first of nine Pro Bowls. In a game Nov. 20, 1977 against the Minnesota Vikings, Payton rushed for a record-setting 275 yards. Also that year, at the age of 23, Payton became the youngest player to be voted the NFL's Most Valuable Player after leading the league with 1,852 rushing yards.

On Oct. 7, 1984, Payton broke Brown's career rushing mark of 12,312 yards with a 6-yard run against the New Orleans Saints. Payton finished that particular game with 154 yards on 32 carries, helping the Bears to a 20-7 triumph.

The 1985 season saw Payton play in and win his only Super Bowl, against the New England Patriots. Oddly enough, even though the game was a blowout (46-10), Payton did not score a touchdown. Prior to the '87 season, Payton signed a $1 million contract for his final campaign as a Bear.

a **Remarkable** run

On Dec. 27, 1987, Payton played his final regular-season game and his No. 34 was retired. In that game he finished with 79 yards and two touchdowns in a loss to the Seattle Seahawks. As a parting gesture, Payton threw two balls into the crowd. "That was just my way of saying thanks," he said. Payton was elected to the Pro Football Hall of Fame in 1993.

One true measure of Sweetness' legacy can be found in the Walter Payton Award, given to the most outstanding offensive performer in Division 1-AA football. This year marks the 12th year of the award, and its presentation will take place Nov. 30 at the Official All-Star Cafe in New York City.

After his playing career ended, Payton, with his restless energy, found much to keep him occupied. He became a partner in a group that unsuccessfully bid to bring a new NFL franchise to St. Louis. Payton also became co-owner of an Indy-Car racing team, Payton/Coyne Racing.

In 1996 Payton and three partners opened Walter Payton's Roadhouse Complex in Aurora, Ill. Once used to repair locomotives, the historic circular building housed America's Brewpub, America's Brewing Co., America's Banquets, The Cognac Cigar Bar and the Walter Payton Museum.

Coach Frank O'Connor said after first seeing
Payton play, "God must have taken a chisel
and said, 'I'm going to make me a halfback.'"

a **Remarkable** run

Bears owner Virginia McCaskey (far right) said, "After Brian Piccolo died, my husband Ed (center) and I promised ourselves we wouldn't be so personally involved with the players. We were able to follow that resolve until Walter Payton came into our lives."

A playful side

During his NFL career, Payton bounced off tacklers and up from being tackled like a superball. In fact, he'd often help the tackler to his feet after delivering the first blow with his signature stiff-arm.

In non-tackling drills, Payton would sometimes break through the line and run backwards, or engage in a dance routine with a defensive back before flipping the ball into an unsuspecting belly. When it was time to rest, he would throw passes on the sideline, often catching the high-velocity 15-yarders with one hand.

When it was a kicker's turn to practice, Payton would shag balls and throw them back at the kicked balls, often hitting them in mid-flight. Once he did it twice in a row, convincing stunned onlookers he could indeed do anything he wanted. If he ever ran out of ideas, he would walk 50 yards down the sideline by himself—on his hands.

In his best games, Payton hoisted the Bears on his shoulder pads and carried them as far as he could. In one

> *If he ever ran out of ideas, he would walk 50 yards down the sideline by himself —on his hands.*

7-0 struggle against the Buffalo Bills, he provided the game's only touchdown by sailing over the Bills' defensive line—another Payton trademark. Buffalo nose tackle Fred Smerlas said, "He was like a fly. I was halfway standing up and he still leaped over my head."

Bud Grant, former coach of the Minnesota Vikings said, "To give you an idea of what the rest of the league thinks about Payton, in our film sessions, our defense actually applauded some of his runs."

Brown said: "I'm a very, very critical individual and I'm only impressed by what I think is greatness. And I saw Walter run two plays and he was the most impressive back that I've seen come into the league in a long time."

Sayers loved what he called Payton's "continuation of the first effort. Some people call it second effort, some call it third effort. If Walter gets hit, people might tend to relax on him. He'll keep driving; he's always trying to squirm out of things."

Payton himself once said he'd like to be remembered along the lines of former Cincinnati Reds star Pete Rose. "Charlie Hustle," Payton said. "Somebody who stands for hard work and total effort. I want to do everything perfectly on the field—pass blocking, running a dummy route, carrying out a fake, all of it."

a Remarkable run

A private side

Payton listed his hobbies as drums and privacy, an odd combination. His wife Connie once told a writer, "He never tells me anything. I almost have to pry everything out of him and I don't think he really likes that, but that's the only way...I don't think a man should keep so much inside. He keeps everything inside and I don't think even Walter's that strong of a person."

Payton was also elusive about the origins of his famous nickname, once giving three different stories in a matter of moments. But whatever the root, "Sweetness" often seemed at odds with Payton's on-field style and intensity.

"He came back to the huddle once after a little 2-yard run and he said, 'Did I hurt him? Did I hurt him?' tackle Ted Albrecht once said. "He makes two yards and wants to know if he punished the guy. That's what makes him a great back."

There was no question that Payton was an ironman; as strong as they come. His running style helped him avoid career-threatening injuries, and his will allowed him to play through the weekly hurts. Payton bent his knees at only a 30-degree angle as opposed to some backs who bend almost 90 degrees. He swung his legs from his hips and ran on his toes, not planting his feet long enough for anyone to get a shot.

Former Bears head coach Mike Ditka called Payton "the greatest Bear of all."

a **Remarkable** run

"Most injuries happen to someone in a relaxed state and Walter's never relaxed," said former Bears conditioning coach Clyde Emrich.

"I think he had a previous life," brother Eddie once told the Chicago Tribune. "He must be the reincarnation of a Great White Shark. If he stops moving forward, he will die."

Tributes

Chicago Mayor Richard Daley proclaimed Nov. 6 as "Walter Payton Day," with a public memorial service at Soldier Field honoring the Bears Hall-of-Famer. The current Bears team, along with Payton's former teammates and fellow NFL players, were present, as was the mayor, the Rev. Jesse Jackson and assorted other speakers.

The Payton family asked the public, in lieu of flowers and donations, to bring a new toy to Soldier Field to be distributed to the Department of Children and Family Services for the holiday season. The toys will be used for the Walter Payton Foundation's "Wishes to Santa Program," benefitting the DCFS.

The private service for Payton was by invitation only and was held Friday, Nov. 5 at noon at Life Changers Church in

---

"If I've done anything that has helped your lives, please use it...I've had a ball and now I'm bowing out."
Walter Payton

South Barrington, Ill. Those wishing to send condolence cards to the Payton family can address them to: Walter Payton Inc., 5407 Trillium, Suite 272, Hoffman Estates, IL., 60192.

In memory of their greatest player, the Chicago Bears now wear a special uniform patch for the remainder of the season in honor of Payton. A small football-shaped cloth piece with an orange "34" set against a dark blue background and worn on the upper-left front side of the jerseys, the patch was unveiled in Green Bay on Nov. 7, as the Bears took on the long-time rival Packers. In their first game since Payton's death, the Bears prevailed in dramatic fashion, a 14-13 squeaker as Chicago blocked a chip-shot field goal attempt by Green Bay's Ryan Longwell as time expired.

Before his final season, in a relaxed moment at the Pro Bowl in Hawaii, Payton "practiced" a retirement speech that now proves as a fitting epitaph: "Chicago, National Football League, world: I am so proud I've had the opportunity to be a part of your lives, to bring some happiness to your lives, and express my talents on the field and off the field.

"And if I've done anything that has helped your lives, please use it. If I've done anything to offend you, please forgive me. I've had a ball and now I'm bowing out."

Pure Sweetness. **34**

Tom Johnson and David Fantle are freelance writers based in Los Angeles and Milwaukee, respectively.

Payton retired after the 1987 season and still holds eight NFL records.

DOUBTERS WERE EVERYWHERE BACK IN 1975. The little running back from little Jackson State couldn t possibly be productive in the big world of the National Football League. Or so they thought.

But Walter Payton s being drafted in the first round was only the start of an entire career of proving people wrong.

I remember reading about him being touted as a Heisman (Trophy) candidate before his senior year in college, said NFL historian Jim Campbell. Almost anybody can be a Heisman candidate, but I thought for somebody coming from Jackson State to be mentioned with the Heisman, this guy has to be something special. And, of course, when he got to the NFL he was more than something special.

That he was. Bears general manager Jim Finks gave him a shot in 1975, and Payton didn t disappoint. What he did do in 13 years in the Windy City was become the greatest football player of all time.

Truly, when all was said and done, Payton s heart and desire are what separated him from everyone else in pads and cleats. He never had the natural ability of a Barry Sanders, the speed or shiftiness of a Gayle Sayers or the brute strength of a Jim Brown. And the best part was that he would be the first to admit there are a host of names in NFL past and present with more pure football talent. But as far as the will to win and desire never to give up, now that was another matter.

To find a task that Walter Payton could not do well on the football field was a lot like trying to find someone who didn t revere him. He had some of his best games rushing when the opposition would crowd the line of scrimmage in an effort to stop the only weapon on some woeful Bears teams. He saw it as a challenge. He also saw it as a challenge to do whatever it took to help his team win. Thing is, he usually did it better than anyone in the business.

Payton possessed some of the best hands the game of football has ever seen. Lost amidst all of his rushing accolades are 492 career receptions for 4,538 yards. His yearly reception total dipped below 27 only once in his career.

Opposing players used to hate to blitz the Bears. Linebackers or safeties would come in looking to level a Bears

When push came to shove, nobody was better

By Trent Modglin

In a class by Himself

quarterback and end up getting leveled themselves. And there would be Payton, lending a hand to help them up off their backs afterward. He was never afraid to sacrifice his body and throw the block that could spring a teammate. In fact, he rather enjoyed it.

"Very few featured backs would actually block back then," said NFL personnel analyst Joel Buchsbaum. "He would occasionally make the really good block and lay into you as opposed to Jim Brown, who took a very indifferent attitude toward blocking. Guys like Brown and O.J. Simpson were not exactly dedicated blockers."

Payton even had to play quarterback for a game in 1984 because the Bears were ravaged by injuries. All he did was toss two touchdowns in eight attempts. In his career, Payton threw 34 passes, eight of which went for scores. Not a bad average.

"To me, he was a throwback," said Campbell. "He was what I remember pro football running backs being like when I was growing up as far as the complete package. He could obviously run, but he could also pass, he could catch, he could block and he could probably play defense if he needed to."

"I looked at Walter differently," said former Bears coach Mike Ditka. "I got as much pleasure watching him block somebody as watching him run for a touchdown. Or watching him catch a pass or throw a pass or kick the ball. He could do it all. In practice he did it as well as most people. He was just a talented guy. He was also the hardest-working guy we had. He was the first guy there and the last to leave. He came to camp in the best shape of anybody that I've seen, and he did it all on his own."

"As a football player, he was really the first running back that I met who I truly respected," said former Bears Hall-of-Fame linebacker Mike Singletary. "He gave me a new respect for running backs. He was the first running back I saw who I thought could have been a really great defensive player."

Oh, and what a free safety or linebacker he

"I got as much pleasure watching him block somebody as watching him run for a touchdown. Or watching him catch a pass or throw a pass or kick the ball. He could do it all."

— *Former Bears coach Mike Ditka*

would have been. It's not often a football player can be compared to someone from the other side of the line of scrimmage, but that's the way he played. Looking back, Payton had enough skill and drive to possibly become the best at several positions—wide receiver, quarterback, fullback, safety—it didn't matter. He would have played them all as hard and perhaps as well as anyone if it meant Chicago had a better chance to win.

But the Bears didn't win very often until later in his career. Many of the Bears teams in the early stages of his career were downright pitiful, and yet there was Payton, stiff-arming and high-stepping his way through opponents who looked like they were trying to stop a truck from rolling down a hill. Bears opponents knew he was going to get the ball, and they still couldn't stop him. Amazingly, Payton never had a year below the 1,200-yard mark on the ground between 1976-86 except for the strike-shortened season of 1982.

"For so many years he was the Bears. Sure, they won the Super Bowl (after the 1985 season), but he was the one bright spot for them in his early years," said Campbell. "He had to go out there on Sundays and know there's not a chance in hell he's going to win this game, but you'd never know it watching him."

The way Payton attacked the game of football with that certain vigor and zest made fans and opponents wonder if he ever bothered to look at the scoreboard. He ran as hard when the Bears were down by 20 as he did if they were up by a field goal late in the game. There were more than enough NFL defenders limping into locker rooms after playing against the Bears to know that Payton enjoyed contact much more than most.

"Walter was always willing to sacrifice on the field for the sake of the team," said former Bears tight end Emery Moorehead. "Ten guys would pile on top of him, and he would be the first guy to get up."

He never ran out of bounds unless he was forced out by two or three players who were bigger and stronger than he was. He didn't believe in it. That was the easy way out and nothing Payton ever did could be described as such. Instead, he lowered a shoulder or his helmet and blasted through would-be tacklers for a few extra yards.

"He basically figured if he hit you harder than you hit him, you would be more likely to back down next time," said Buchsbaum.

"No one can ever question the heart because there are too many film clips where he appears to be tackled and ends up getting 40 more yards," said Campbell.

It was a style of play that often had opposing crowds cheering. It was a level of respect, and Walter made it acceptable to go all out all the time. He also set a standard for durability.

Payton missed one game in his entire career. It came during his rookie year and the injury left him in tears because he couldn't play and couldn't help his team. That's how much the game meant to him. He carried the ball on 3,838 occasions, threw thousands of blocks, got punished by linemen in 189 NFL games and missed only one. And he desperately wanted to play in that game, but his coaches wouldn't let him.

When historians and experts and fans begin to look for candidates for that contrived title of "the

continued on page 26

"For so many years he was the Bears. Sure, they won the Super Bowl in '85, but he was the one bright spot for them in his early years."

— *NFL historian Jim Campbell*

Walter Payton Career Statistics

Regular Season

Rushing / Receiving

Year	No.	Yds.	Avg.	LG	TD	No.	Yds.	Avg.	LG	TD	G/GS
1975	196	679	3.5	54	7	33	213	6.5	40	0	13/7
1976	311	1,390	4.5	60	13	14	149	9.9	34	0	14/14
1977	339	1,852	5.5	73	14	27	269	10.0	75	2	14/14
1978	333	1,395	4.2	76	11	50	480	9.5	61	0	16/16
1979	369	1,610	4.4	43	14	31	313	10.1	65	2	16/16
1980	317	1,460	4.6	69	6	46	367	8.0	54	1	16/16
1981	339	1,222	3.6	39	6	41	379	9.2	30	2	16/16
1982	148	596	4.0	26	1	32	311	9.7	40	0	9/9
1983	314	1,421	4.5	49	6	53	607	11.5	74	2	16/16
1984	381	1,684	4.4	72	11	45	368	8.2	31	0	16/16
1985	324	1,551	4.8	40	9	49	483	9.9	65	1	16/16
1986	321	1,333	4.2	41	8	37	382	10.3	57	1	16/16
1987	146	533	3.7	17	4	33	217	6.6	16	1	12/12
Total	**3,838**	**16,726**	**4.4**	**76**	**110**	**492**	**4,542**	**9.1**	**75**	**15**	**190/184**

Career Passing: 11-34-331, 8 TD, 5 Int.
Career Kickoff Returns: 17 for 539 yds. (31.7 avg.)
Career Punting: 1 for 39 yds.

Playoffs

Rushing

Year	No.	Yds.	Avg.	LG	TD
1977	19	60	3.1	11	0
1979	16	67	4.2	12	2
1984	46	196	4.3	20	0
1985	67	186	2.8	12	0
1986	14	38	2.7	9	0
1987	18	85	4.7	16	0
Total	**180**	**632**	**3.5**	**20**	**2**

Receiving

No.	Yds.	Avg.	LG	TD	G/GS
3	33	11.0	20	0	1/1
3	52	17.3	31	0	1/1
4	23	5.8	12	0	2/2
8	52	6.5	19	0	3/3
1	-2	-2.0	-2	0	1/1
3	20	6.7	9	0	1/1
22	**178**	**8.3**	**31**	**0**	**9/9**

Also: 3 kickoff returns for 57 yards (1977)

continued from page 23

best football player in history," there's no doubt that the names of several quality players come to mind. Brown is one, but it can be argued that he didn't want to be the complete player and that he was doing everything really before his time, dominating when no one else was around to stop him, a la Wilt Chamberlain of the NBA. Joe Montana and Jerry Rice exploited defenses for a decade like no other quarterback/wide receiver tandem in the history of the game and won a pair of Super Bowls together in the process. But at no fault of their own, one could say that Rice helped make Montana or vice versa, or perhaps that the Bill Walsh West Coast offense made it possible for both of them to thrive. Marion Motley and Paul Hornung are names that also surface, but would they have thrived on the Bears' offense of the late '70s or against the defenses Payton battled on a regular basis? Not likely.

So the debate for the ages circles back around to Sweetness, and all of a sudden the critics can't be heard from, other than the fact he wasn't the strongest or fastest. They can't come up with something, anything, that could hold Payton back from the title of the NFL's greatest player in spite of the fact he may not have even been the greatest running back of all time.

"If I could pick any backfield, I would pick Jim Brown and I'd have to have Walter Payton in there with him," said another NFL historian, Bob Carroll. "I'd have to." Sweetness holds the NFL rushing record, the record for combined net yardage, for most games with 100 or more yards on the

ground (77), most rushing yards gained in a game (275) and is tied with Sanders for seasons with at least 1,000 yards rushing (10).

"He was the best football player I've ever seen, and probably one of the best people I've ever met," said Ditka. "It's really sad to me. But the first thought I had of him was not sadness. It was of all the great things he meant to the city of Chicago and the Bears and the fans. To watch him play was pretty special."

"He was unique, and whenever I put together an All-Time team, I rate Jim Brown the greatest running back, but it really hurts to leave someone like Payton off and not rate him the best," said Campbell. "I'm not so sure 11 Walter Paytons couldn't beat 11 Jim Browns, or anybody else for that matter."

It may not have even been a close game. **34**

Trent Modglin is an editor at Pro Football Weekly, based in suburban Chicago.

Career Highlights

1975 — First-round pick in NFL Draft (4th overall) by the Chicago Bears.

1977 — Rushed for NFL single-game record 275 yards against Minnesota on Novermber 20.

1977 — Won NFL Most Valuable Player award with 1,852 rushing yards, 14 rushing touchdowns and a 5.5 yards-per-carry average, all career highs.

1984 — Broke Jim Brown's long-standing career rushing record in a game against New Orleans.

1985 — Won second MVP award after rushing for 1,551 yards and nine touchdowns for Super Bowl champions.

1987 — Retired from football as the owner of eight NFL records, including the all-time rushing record (16,726 yards), most combined net yards gained in a career (21,803), most yards in a single game (275), most seasons with 1,000 or more yards rushing (10) and most rushing attempts (3,838). Also holds 28 Bears records. Voted to nine Pro Bowls (1976-80, 1983-86).

1993 — Voted into Pro Football Hall of Fame on January 30 (inducted July 31). Named his son, Jarrett, to be the first son to present his father for induction into the Hall.

"He was the best football player I've ever seen, and probably one of the best people I've ever met."

— *Mike Ditka*

A Little

"I can give the man the smallest crack in the line and Walter will make two miles out of it."

— *Bears teammate Noah Jackson*

Piece of Light

By Roland Lazenby

A LARGE PART OF THE context for a professional life well-lived includes all those Bears teams of the 1970s. Remember them? Remember Bob Avellini, Vince Evans, Kenny Margerum and Brian Baschnagel? Remember all the losses? All those cold, empty Sunday afternoons at Soldier Field?

Bears football in the 1970s wasn't so much a free-fall as it was a sort of hopeless, miserable exercise.

Then came Walter Payton. A first-round pick in 1975. He rushed eight times in his first game and finished with zero yards. Observers said there were tears in his eyes when he walked off the field that day.

From there he proceeded to carve out a reputation for himself on the NFL's toughest proving ground, the muddy, icy, slippery fields of the NFC Central. For the most part, his was a bad-weather opera. Payton had a bum ankle that rookie year and sat out one game due to a coach's decision. From that point on, he played in 184 consecutive games. In 13 years, he missed one game, that coach's decision his rookie season.

It was in his third year of competition that he set the gemstone on which the rest of his career would be built, that dreamlike 1977 campaign when the Bears hitched onto Payton's determination and turned a 3-5 start into a 9-6 trip to the playoffs and league MVP honors for Payton himself.

For obvious reasons, the big day was Nov. 20, 1977, when Chicago offered its best bluster, cold winds whipping off Lake Michigan and gray clouds hanging thick with the threat of snow and freezing rain.

Payton had the flu. "During introductions, I was weak," he said.

How bad were the conditions? Even the noise from the throng at Soldier Field was strangely muffled. Too cold to clap.

Payton ran 40 times that day for an NFL single-game record 275 yards, and that prodigious productivity was just enough for the Bears to grunt out a 10-7 win over the Minnesota Vikings.

Series after series, he rolled out for that Bears sweep behind Revie Sorey. Time after time, he took on tacklers, the shoulder lowered, the knees kicking high. It was an image of relentless effort that he struck in the minds of his opponents, his fans, his teammates.

"I can give the man the smallest crack in the line and Walter will make two miles out of it," said Bears guard Noah Jackson. "The smallest crack, a little piece of light."

Vikings coach Bud Grant watched Payton with admiration that day, and many others watched him struggle and succeed despite being allied with anemic Bears passing games run by the likes of Avellini, Evans and Mike Phipps, despite the messy fields and slippery footing.

"As far as an opponent for the Vikings, Payton was No. 1. He was the whole package—runner, of course, but also a great blocker and pass receiver," said Grant upon the news of Payton's death. "My criteria was that, to be a great player, you also had to play...had to be out there every week. Walter didn't play on very good teams, but he didn't miss a game, and he gave it everything he had to the last play, even if the Bears were losing by two or three touchdowns."

That passion spoke for itself in 1993 when the Hall of Fame's voters were considering Payton's worthiness for the honor. Charged with making a nomination, Chicago voter Cooper Rollow decided to pass, telling the selectors instead that his prepared speech couldn't begin to address Payton's greatness as a player.

"Was it unanimous?" Payton asked after the secret vote, a question that took interviewers by surprise. Asked to explain his concern, Payton said, "I try to be the best I possibly can. If I do it, I do it all the way. If I get in unanimously, it means I was recognized as the best. If I didn't get in unanimously, I know I wasn't."

The numbers, of course, did their speaking for Payton. Thirteen seasons as a running back for the Bears, seasons which produced records such as yards rushing (16,726) and rushing touchdowns (110). Sweetness also had 4,538 yards in receptions, had an NFL record of 21,803 combined net yards. He won the NFC rushing title five consecutive years from 1976-80, played in nine Pro Bowl games and was named NFL Player of the Year in 1977 and '85.

He rushed for 1,000 or more yards in 10 of his 13 seasons and had a league-record 77 games of 100 or more yards rushing.

"It's grossly unfair to judge Walter Payton solely on the yards he gained," former Bears general manager Jim Finks said upon Payton's Hall of Fame selection. "He is a complete football player, better than Jim Brown, better than O.J. Simpson."

It was important to Payton that this evaluation be based simply on his football deeds. The fact that he was a warm, wonderful person off the field should not enter into the picture. It had to be unanimous. Complete.

And that, of course, was his reward. His performances left no questions, not in the minds of those who were there, who really knew, who saw him turn those little pieces of light into that burning fire. 34

Roland Lazenby is the author of more than 40 sports books.

Sweet
Memories

Sweet Memories

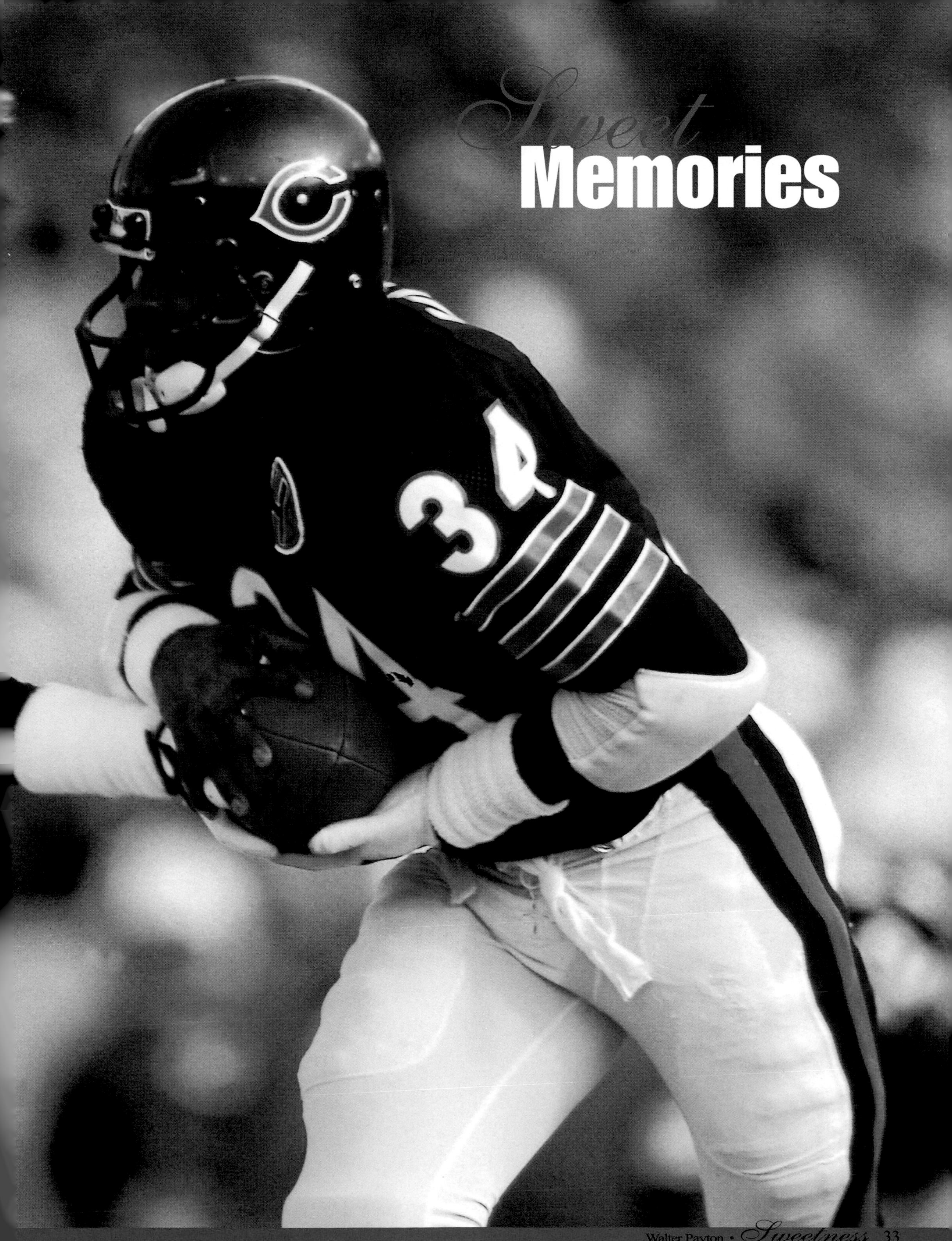

Sweet
Memories

Sweet **Memories**

Sweet
Memories

Sweet Memories

Sweet
Memories

Quotables

Heard around the NFL and beyond:

Fox analyst and former Raiders head coach John Madden:

"He was a guy who was special. I think of all the guys that I covered over the years, and he was my favorite. He epitomized what a football player was and he epitomized what Chicago was and what a Bear was. They can talk about Michael Jordan and Mike Ditka and Sammy Sosa, but Walter Payton was Chicago sports."

Former Chicago Bull Michael Jordan:

"Walter was a Chicago icon long before I arrived there. He was a great man off the field and his on-the-field accomplishments speak for them-selves. I spent a lot of time with Walter, and I truly feel that we have lost a great man."

Former Steelers RB Franco Harris:

"As far as I'm concerned, I thought he was the greatest. With the teams he played on, and what he did, missing only one game his whole career...And, on top of that, he was just a great guy."

Dolphins QB Dan Marino:

"When I came into the league I looked up to him, not only as a player, but how he handled him-self as a person. He will be missed by everyone who was fortunate to have known him."

Colts head coach Jim Mora:

"He was a great guy, a great human being, a very giving person. It's a real tragedy. We've lost a great man and one of the all-time great football players in the National Football League."

Chargers QB Jim Harbaugh, a former teammate of Payton's:

"He meant so much to the city of Chicago. 'Sweetness'—there may not have been a better nickname for a player."

Vikings head coach Dennis Green:

"He set a standard for going all out. He wasn't as big as some of your other backs that play the game, but he could outwork anybody and he always gave 100 percent. And that was 100 percent to his family, to his friends, to the game of football, and so he is a guy that is really going to be missed."

NFL commissioner Paul Tagliabue:

"All of us in the NFL family are saddened by the loss of Walter Payton. He was without a doubt one of the greatest players in the history of the sport. Walter exemplified class and all of us in sports should honor him by striving to perpetuate his standard of excellence. Walter was an inspiration in everything he did. The tremendous grace and dignity he displayed in his final months reminded us again why 'Sweetness' was the perfect nickname for Walter Payton."

Quotables

Former Dolphins head coach Don Shula:

"The thing I remember most about Payton was that he brought everything he had to the game. He was such a complete back, there was no weakness. One word comes to mind when setting up the game plan for Walter Payton: Respect. You respected him for being a great runner, a great blocker and a great pass receiver. A guy who was always going to be out there, being the true superstar that he is. He was always a gentleman and a family man, all the things you admire in a person."

Former Bears head coach Mike Ditka (now with New Orleans):

"He was the best football player I've ever seen. It's sad to me because he had a lot greater impact on me than I had on him. And he led by example on the field. He was the complete player. He did everything. He was the greatest runner, but he was also probably the best blocking back you ever saw. I got as much pleasure out of watching him block somebody. He could do it all, yet also he was the hardest-working guy we had. He came to camp in the best shape of anyone I'd seen."

Former Bears LB Doug Buffone:

"In his very first practice, Walter gets the ball and comes right at me and runs me over. He does the same thing the very next play. I wasn't going to let it happen the next time. He comes at me and I hit him as hard as I can. He pops up and the next snap, here he comes again. I knew right then and there that he was a special player. He was relentless from the very beginning and that's the way he played his entire career."

Former Vikings DT Alan Page:

"Walter Payton was not only a great football player, he was one of the great people of our time. His football talent speaks for itself, but what most people do not know is his incredible humanity, his wonderful sense of humor and his love for children. His true legacy will be found in his children and family."

Former Vikings DE Jim Marshall:

"What you remember is the tenacity with which he approached each and every play. If you didn't wrap him up and put him down, he had a chance to score a touchdown."

Buffalo QB Doug Flutie, a former teammate of Payton's:

"During the playoffs, he'd pull my socks down in the huddle. When I was in Chicago, it was kind of a hostile atmosphere and Walter was one of my closest friends on the team. It was a privilege to play with him and I knew it at the time. I think Walter thought it was a matter of him getting a liver transplant and him being Walter again. A lot of people believed that, including me. He was going to be Walter all over again."

Cowboys RB Emmitt Smith:

"I feel empty. There's no other way to describe it. This is a great loss. Walter Payton was an inspiration to me, by the way he carried himself."

Former Vikings head coach Bud Grant:

"Heroes don't last very long. But in my book Walter Payton was the greatest running back in the league."

Compiled by Steve Silverman

Steve Silverman is the national correspondent for College and Pro Football Newsweekly, and has served in that role for the last three years. Prior to that, he was a senior editor at Pro Football Weekly for 10 years. Silverman is also a columnist for Pro Sports Xchange. He has won three writing awards from the Pro Football Writers of America.

Destiny calls

There was no stopping Payton and the '85 Bears

By Bob LeGere

BY 1985 WALTER PAYTON HAD ALREADY BECOME THE NO. 1 ground gainer in the history of the NFL, having surpassed Jim Brown's record of 12,312 yards the previous season en route to his career total of 16,726.

He had led the NFC in rushing yardage five straight seasons and guaranteed his place in the Pro Football Hall of Fame. Nine times he had run for over 1,000 yards in a season. Payton had already accumulated most of his 21,803 combined yards, more than anyone who ever played the game.

But Payton had never been a member of a world champion, and that was what he wanted most. It wasn't until his 10th season in 1984, months after Payton had surpassed Brown's career rushing record, that he played in his first winning playoff game, a 23-19 defeat of the Redskins in Washington.

After that victory, all that stood between the Bears and a Super Bowl berth was the San Francisco 49ers. The rushing record was nice, but it wasn't enough to satisfy Payton.

"If that would have been my goal, all I dreamed of, then I would've walked off the field after that game (against the Saints on Oct. 7, 1984) and took my cape off," he said. "My goal was to go beyond that."

But the following week, when the Bears were eliminated by San Francisco in the NFC championship game (23-0) to conclude their 1984 season, Payton was so distraught he at first refused to join his teammates for the return flight to Chicago. He had to be talked on board by the team's chairman of the board, Ed McCaskey.

The taunting words of the 49ers, especially safety Ronnie Lott, had cut Payton like a dull dagger. "Next time bring your offense," Lott chided the beaten Bears as they slumped off the field.

linebackers Mike Singletary and Otis Wilson.

In '85 Payton was one of many stars, and he was content as always to fade into the background, maintaining the privacy that he cherished, even though he was as outgoing and personable as any superstar has ever been. There was no mistaking his importance to the team, though. He may have been overlooked by some in favor of more outrageous teammates, but Payton remained the focal point of the offense

Despite Payton's presence, the Bears had been shut out, playing without quarterback Jim McMahon, who had suffered a lacerated kidney earlier in the season. Although Payton rushed for 92 yards on 22 carries against the Niners, backup quarterback Steve Fuller managed just 87 passing yards while completing 13 of 22 passes.

The next season would be different. By 1985 Payton no longer had to carry the Bears on his shoulders as he had for so many years, running the ball more times than anyone in NFL history. Payton finally had a Pro Bowl-caliber quarterback in McMahon to complement him. The Bears also had a suffocating defense that was capable of winning games by thoroughly dominating opponents.

Media and fans alike were captivated by the eclectic collection of stars ranging from the punky, anti-establishment McMahon to the sideshow attraction William "Refrigerator" Perry, the 300-plus-pound rookie defensive tackle/fullback/running back/pass receiver.

After the '85 season, Payton was joined on the eighth of his nine Pro Bowl trips by eight teammates: McMahon; offensive tackle Jim Covert; defensive ends Richard Dent and Dan Hampton; safety Dave Duerson; center Jay Hilgenberg and

in 1985, rushing for 1,551 yards, the fourth-best season of his 13-year career. His 4.8-yard average per carry was the second-best single-season mark of his career.

"I don't care how well McMahon plays," said Hampton, "Payton's still the heart and soul of that offense."

Because no running back had ever played at such a high level for so long, some assumed that after 10 years Payton must surely have been slowing down. "I hear people say he's lost a step," fullback Matt Suhey said during the '85 season. "That's pure bull. He's absolutely as good as he's ever been. He's probably contributing as much as he ever has, but he doesn't have the ball doing it. He picks up blitzes, blocks as well, runs great pass patterns. Anything they're asking him to do, he does."

Destiny
calls

Destiny
Destiny
Destiny
Destiny
Destiny
Destiny
Destiny
Destiny
Destiny
Destiny
Destiny

As always, Payton's contribution to the Bears went well beyond rushing yards, pass receptions, touchdowns and blocks. His behind-the-scenes work on the Super Bowl XX championship team was crucial to a team chemistry that was volatile and always a threat to explode. A fault line had developed between the offense and the defense. That was evident even after the Bears destroyed the Patriots 46-10 in the Super Bowl. Defensive coordinator Buddy Ryan was carried off the field by his players, while head coach Mike Ditka was hoisted on the shoulders of the offense. Shortly thereafter Ditka and Ryan split up, with the defensive guru becoming the Eagles' head coach.

Payton more than any other player helped keep both sides of the ball together as the rift between Ditka and Ryan widened. "I think he was the one guy that really worked hard at pulling that team together in the '80s when it could have come apart," Ditka said. "We were kind of a faction of offense and defense, and he really worked hard at pulling it together and got each side to respect each other. We finally became a football team instead of an offense and a defense."

Both sides of the ball were superb in Week

McMahon (left) had a knack for stealing the headlines in '85, but it was Payton's second MVP performance that fueled the offense.

Destiny
calls

Destiny
Destiny
Destiny
Destiny
Destiny
Destiny
Destiny
Destiny
Destiny
Destiny
Destiny

Six of that championship season. That was the first big test for the Bears, a return trip to Candlestick Park, where they had been humiliated to end the previous season. Payton carried the day for the Bears—and the ball, 24 times for 132 yards. On a drive late in the fourth quarter, he carried nine times for 52 yards, scoring from 17 yards out to cap a 26-10 victory.

"Unfortunately, when the 49ers beat us last year, they didn't show much courtesy or dignity," said Payton, who won the League's MVP award in '85. "They said negative things about our offense after shutting us out. We thought about that all during the off-season. A team of All-Pros couldn't have stopped us."

For Payton, known for being gracious in victory or defeat, those were harsh words. His way was to win the war on the field, not the war of words. The victory over San Francisco gave the Bears a 6-0 record, and, more importantly, an attitude, the result of having destroyed their destroyer. In earlier games that season the Bears had proved they could win without Payton playing a huge role, but even when he wasn't the main attraction No. 34 had shown his versatility. In a 45-10 blowout of the Redskins in Week Four, Payton had just six yards on seven carries,

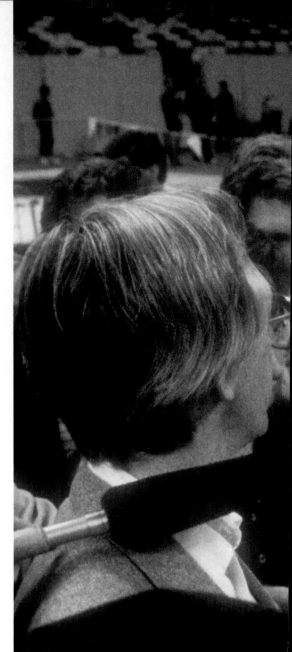

Perry was the center of the media's attention in the days leading up to Super Bowl XX in New Orleans.

Destiny
Destiny
Destiny
calls
Destiny
Destiny
Destiny
Destiny
Destiny
Destiny
Destiny
Destiny
Destiny
Destiny

his lowest rushing total in four years. But he threw a TD pass to McMahon, the eighth of his career. The previous week, in a nationally televised game against the Vikings on a Thursday night, McMahon came off the bench to throw three TD passes in less than seven minutes. Payton's spectacular pickup of a blitzing linebacker allowed McMahon to throw a 70-yard score to Willie Gault to start the comeback.

Three more victories followed the watershed win over the Niners, complete with three more 100-yard rushing days for Payton. Two of the wins were against the hated Packers, the second one, in Week Nine, a bitter and brutal 16-10 win at Lambeau Field.

Early in the game Packers cornerback Mark Lee rode Payton out of bounds, over the bench and into the stadium wall. Later, Suhey, was buried by safety Ken Stills as he stood on the outskirts of a pileup several moments after the play had been whistled dead. While the cheap shots and trash-talking flowed freely, Payton retaliated as he usually did, with 192 yards on 28 carries. Playing the role of Mr. Diplomacy, Sweetness refused to accuse the Packers of dirty play when he was asked if they had tried to purposely injure him.

"I don't think so," he said. "(Packers coach) Forrest Gregg was a class player."

Payton's 27-yard TD run in the fourth quarter was the Bears' only touchdown and kept them perfect at 9-0. The run could have been stopped near the line of scrimmage, and if it were almost any other running back it would have been. Packers linebacker Brian Noble unloaded a

Payton did his share of celebrating during the 15-1 regular season in 1985. His 1,551-yard rushing total was the fourth-highest of his 13-year career.

Destiny
Destiny
Destiny
calls
Destiny
Destiny
Destiny
Destiny
Destiny
Destiny
Destiny
Destiny
Destiny
Destiny

vicious hit on Payton, which knocked him backward, but he bounced off and outran the defense to the end zone.

"I knocked the crap out of Payton," Noble said. "He's such a good athlete that he just kept going."

Added Ditka: "I thought Payton's exhibition was maybe as good as I've ever seen a guy with a football under his arm play."

Three more lopsided victories followed—24-3 over the Lions, 44-0 against the Cowboys and 36-0 over the Falcons—paced by three more 100-yard-plus efforts from Payton. That gave him a record ninth 1,000-yard season and his seventh straight 100-yard game, tying the record held by O.J. Simpson and Earl Campbell.

The blowout of the Cowboys erased any doubt about the legitimacy of the Bears' title aspirations. It also provided a moment of comic relief amid the destruction of America's Team. Payton, who rushed for 132 yards on his own, got a helping hand from Perry near the goal line when the rookie picked him up and attempted to carry him into the end zone.

"I didn't know what was going on," said Payton. The officials did, and Perry was penalized.

The victory over the Falcons the following week gave the Bears a 12-0 record as they became only the third team in NFL history to win 12 games to start a season. It was an unlucky 13th for the Bears, though, as they were ambushed 38-24 by the Dolphins on a Monday night, despite 121 yards from Payton. Although the chance for a perfect season had evaporated, Ditka was still full of praise for the continuing excellence provided by Payton.

"Walter Payton is the greatest football player to ever play the game," the coach said. "Other people who call themselves running backs can't carry his jersey."

The Bears rebounded with three more wins to finish the season

The Patriots held Payton to 61 yards in the Super Bowl and even forced an early fumble that led to a short-lived 3-0 lead.

Destiny
Destiny
Destiny
calls
Destiny
Destiny
Destiny
Destiny
Destiny
Destiny
Destiny
Destiny
Destiny

15-1. Payton stretched his 100-yard streak to nine games, and even when it ended in a 19-6 victory over the Jets he contributed a TD by taking a swing pass and going 65 yards for a score.

The entire post-season run for the '85 Bears was as anticlimactic as most of the 33 Super Bowls have been. The Bears blanked the Giants 21-0 and the Rams 24-0 at Soldier Field before ending Chicago's 22-year title-less drought with the rout of the Patriots at the Superdome in New Orleans.

Although it was the culmination of 11 years of tireless work by Payton, the Bears didn't need him to produce the huge numbers as he had so often in the past. After gaining 93 yards against the Giants, Payton managed just 32 yards on 18 carries versus the Rams and 61 yards on 22 attempts against the Pats. He also lost a fumble in that game that led to the Patriots taking a short-lived 3-0 lead.

Payton didn't score at all in the postseason, and when the rookie Perry was given the ball from one yard out for the final Bears touchdown of the Super Bowl, the most prolific runner in NFL history couldn't hide his disappointment.

Ditka and McMahon were both blamed for failing to get Payton the touchdown that he wanted so badly and both regretted not doing their part to make it happen. But others thought Payton overreacted and appeared selfish for worrying about personal accomplishments in a team victory. Those who knew Payton realized it was more his tremendous pride than selfishness that accounted for his displeasure over not getting into the end zone.

"It definitely let the air out of my balloon at that particular time," he would say later. "But I became more mature about life and things, and I said to myself, 'If scoring a touchdown in the Super Bowl was the ultimate that made my career great, then obviously, whatever I did in the past didn't mean anything.' So that's the way I looked at it.'"

Payton said he was more disappointed by the failure of the big game to live up to his expectations than he was over being kept out of the end zone. "I was expecting the Super Bowl to be the greatest game I ever played," said Payton, "but on a scale of 1 to 10, I'd give it a 2. If it had been 14-12, maybe it would have meant more."

Center Jay Hilgenberg cut through all the debate and got right to the heart of the matter. "He's the greatest," said Hilgenberg. "He doesn't need a Super Bowl touchdown to be the greatest."

Ditka, who coached Payton in his final six seasons, agreed with Hilgenberg. He knew how integral Payton was to his world-championship team.

"Walter Payton is the greatest football player I've ever seen," said Ditka. "He was the best disciplined athlete I've ever been around, and he was fun to be with. He did everything we asked, and we asked him to do everything." **34**

Bob LeGere is the Bears beat writer for the Daily Herald in Arlington Heights, Ill., where he has covered the Bears for the past eight years. He previously worked for nine years at Pro Football Weekly.

Payton is credited with keeping the Ryan-led defense (right) and the Ditka-led offense from splitting too far apart during the title run.

Destiny
Destiny
Destiny
calls
Destiny
Destiny
Destiny
Destiny
Destiny
Destiny

**'85
Bears**

Losing
The '85 Bears

By Bob LeGere

Former teammates remember so much more about Walter Payton than the thousands of tackles he ran through with his unique combination of strength, speed, grace and determination; the blocks he threw that flattened much bigger players, and the durability that allowed him to start 186 games at the most demanding position on the field.

"I will always remember his smile," said Hall-of-Fame middle linebacker Mike Singletary, who was there with Payton on the Monday morning of his death. "He loved to laugh, he loved to have fun. You couldn't believe a guy who was as great as he was had that much humor and wouldn't take himself seriously."

Singletary was there by Payton's bedside in the final days, praying with and for the man he played with for seven years. When it was over, Singletary cried for himself, for his loss, but not for Payton, who died with all the grace that he played with.

"I think outside of anything else I've seen—the greatest run, the greatest moves—what I experienced this weekend was by far the best of Walter Payton that I had seen," Singletary said. "When I left him (Monday) morning, I remember going home and telling my wife that there was a peace that surpassed all understanding when I looked at him. There was a peace there I had definitely not seen all year."

Teammates who remembered Payton in his playing days as nothing short of Superman had difficulty believing that his illness, regardless of the severity, could defeat him.

"When you played with him, you recognized the guy as invincible," said wide receiver Dennis McKinnon. That perception never died.

"I think we all thought in the back of our minds, when this was announced months ago," said kicker Kevin Butler, "that this would be another thing that Walter would overcome because of him being Walter Payton. I think we all believed that nothing could stop this guy."

"It's devastating," said Arizona Cardinals defensive coordinator Dave McGinnis, the Bears linebackers coach near the end of Payton's playing career. "It's a hard thing for me to imagine Walter being gone because he was so much alive when he was there. Nobody embodied life more than Walter Payton."

McGinnis commiserated with Johnny Roland, the Bears' running backs coach in Payton's prime.

"We sat and looked at each other and we both cried," McGinnis said. "It's hard to imagine that he's gone."

While the liver disease, primary sclerosing cholangitis, and the resulting bile duct cancer sapped Payton's strength and size, it never diminished his sense of humor, which was as legendary as his football talents.

"He was the kind of individual who, if you were down, he would not let you remain down," said Singletary. "It was his duty to bring humor and life in any situation."

Fullback Matt Suhey was a constant visitor to Payton's home in the final months, making sure he got out to see old friends and teammates. Suhey was one of Payton's closest friends since their playing days when he often led the way for what would become highlight-film runs. That also made Suhey one of Payton's favorite targets for pranks.

Just weeks before his death, Payton told Suhey he wanted to visit Singletary. Suhey drove, Payton navigated.

"Is this Mike Singletary's house?" Suhey inquired of an elderly woman after pulling up to the address Payton had given him.

"Mike *who*?" she said.

Suhey's deathly ill friend pulled the same stunt a couple more times. Each time Suhey fell for it, and each time when he returned to the car, there was Payton, having one last laugh. 34

Heart of Gold

Payton's greatness matched only by his generosity

By Aaron George

WALTER PAYTON HAD A knack for lighting up children's eyes as soon as he entered a room. He owned a repertoire off the field that was every bit as devastating to sadness and gloom as his straight-arm and high-step were to opposing defenders on the field. He had that playful smile, that penchant for boyish pranks, that uncommon ability to relate to anyone no matter how desperate their situation. Children who met "Sweetness" knew they had been touched by an uncommon person—a person who didn't need to spend so much of his time helping "common" people, but who couldn't have imagined living any other way.

What the children didn't know was that much of Payton's life, including the final days before his passing on Nov. 1, 1999—All Saints' Day—was dedicated to ensuring their happiness even when he couldn't be there in person.

The Walter Payton Foundation was the primary way this was accomplished. In 1989 Payton, encouraged by the family of legendary Bears owner George Halas, established the George Halas/Walter Payton Foundation. The organization, which was changed to The Walter Payton Foundation in 1998, was founded to provide "financial and motivational support to youth, and to help them realize that they can raise the quality of their lives, and the lives of those around them."

The founder embodied this mission. He chose to deflect attention away from himself and his celebrity status and give it to those who really needed it: children. He did this in countless ways, most of which were unbeknownst to the public while he was still alive. Only recently, since Payton deemed it beneficial to the Foundation, has the true scope of his kindness been revealed.

For years Sweetness organized a Christmas drive—the "Wishes for Santa Program"—which brought toys and clothes to underprivileged youth throughout Illinois. By his own choice, few recognized his generosity. He opted to remain anonymous to the children in this massive undertaking, which resulted in the donation of 35,000 gift bags on Christmas Day, 1998. The bags, each filled with about $100 worth of clothes and toys, went to children who spent the holidays away from their families

"What people know is that Walter represents credibility. They knew that when Walter did something, he was going to do it 100 times better than even he said he was going to do it."
— Kim Tucker, Executive Director of the Walter Payton Foundation

"I think children could sense that Walter loved them so much. They literally would go up and hug him or run up and grab his leg."
— Kim Tucker

in the care of the Department of Children and Family Services (DCFS).

"The children thought that Santa Claus was the one bringing the toys," said Kim Tucker, executive director of the Payton Foundation. "These were children who normally didn't get Christmas presents, and they thought that Santa wouldn't come because they did something wrong. Walter wanted them to have happy childhood memories; he wanted them to have self-esteem and self-respect."

Jeanie Ortega-Piron, legal guardian for children at the DCFS, said the Payton Foundation has been a godsend.

"They've been the best thing that happened to us," she told the Chicago Tribune. "Last year, we turned our entire gift program over to them."

As was his legacy, Payton's annual drive involved the entire community. Two thousand volunteer caretakers were required to distribute the gift packages, which remained out of the children's sight until Christmas morning, when they awoke to a boisterous yuletide cheer. Large corporations such as Levi Strauss, Fischer Price and Hasbro gave generously with little to gain for themselves. The business world was also quick to help fund other Payton Foundation programs, including a job placement program for struggling 18- to 21-year-olds, and sports memorabilia auctions that donated proceeds to over 9,000 churches and social service agencies.

"What people know is that Walter represents credibility," said Tucker. "They knew that when Walter did something, he was going to do it 100 times better than even he said he was going to do it. So these corporations had no hesitation in coming forward, even though they didn't gain much publicity by doing so."

Though unmistakable to those who were close to him, Payton's spiritual side also remained shrouded from the public. Friends say God was the driving force behind his selfless passion for helping others. "We looked creatively for ways that we could make the wishes of these children come true, and we prayed to God a lot, and it always happened," said Tucker, who's worked for the organization since 1993. "We both believed that our foundation was ordained by God, and it didn't take a tremendous amount of donations to make it successful."

If kindness and spirituality were Payton's bread, his butter was a lively sense of humor, which managed to touch almost everyone at some point. Verified stories abound of the wild pranks he pulled on friends, teammates, media members and strangers. But when matters of the Foundation were concerned, Sweetness quickly shifted to his serious side.

"Walter was very intense and very serious when it came to the foundation," said Tucker, who, like all members of the organization, is an unpaid volunteer. "He felt that he wanted to represent the children, and he brought a lot of fun into their lives. And he never forgot about that even when it came to his business ventures."

But Payton had an ability to turn even the most serious circumstance into an opportunity for fun and games. In public outings, droves of children would huddle around him, latch onto his arms and legs, laughing hysterically. He would sign autographs and exchange stories with random kids and adults alike. He was often able to recall conversations he'd had with strangers several years prior. Even in his final days, with the implications of his illness weighing heavily, he found time for people, particularly children. He threw out the first pitch at the Cubs' home opener in April, and he later addressed the media to raise awareness of the need for organ donors.

"I think children could sense that Walter loved them so much," said Tucker. "They literally would go up and hug him or run up and grab his leg. And these kids didn't know who he was; they just loved being around him."

All that said, many still call it a coincidence that Walter Payton passed from this world on All Saints' Day. Thousands of children know better. 34

To learn more about the Walter Payton Foundation, visit www.payton34.com.

The Softer Side of Sweetness

Off the field, he left his mark on family, friends and teammates

By Don Pierson

WALTER PAYTON TOUCHED more than a football. Every teammate, every person he met, has a story.

"He was one of the most physical persons I was ever around. He had to touch you. He had to engage you," said Gary Fencik, Payton's teammate for 12 years. "He couldn't just walk up and say, 'Hi, I'm Walter Payton.' He had to pick you up off the ground and almost break your ribs."

His handshake would bring you to your knees. He would pinch, grab, bite, squeeze. It was all in fun, of course. To him, it was playful, not painful. Payton demanded everyone around him have as much fun as he was having.

"He wouldn't let you be sad," said Mike Singletary, a teammate who prayed with Payton on his last day.

Payton's grip on football extended beyond Chicago. In a poll of 200 rookies drafted in 1999, Payton was the overwhelming choice as "Greatest All-Time NFL Player." Payton got 64 votes, far more than Joe Montana (18), Jerry Rice (17), Lawrence Taylor (15) or Jim Brown (13). True, the poll reflects its youthful audience, but Payton is more ancient history to today's rookies than Montana, Rice or Taylor.

What made Payton so popular and memorable was that he was down to earth in more ways than his prodigious 16,726 yards rushing. "I never felt Walter thought he was better than anyone else," said Singletary. "I never felt any arrogance. Never. And that's special."

There is a difference between ego and arrogance, and it's not even a very fine line. Payton once explained: "I don't perceive myself as being better than anyone. I shovel my driveway. I go to the grocery store. I pump my own gas. Some athletes don't do that."

It appears Payton and unassuming wife Connie passed the humility down to their son and daughter. "These last 12 months have been extremely tough on me and my family, but through these difficult times we've learned a lot about love and life," said

The Softer Side of Sweetness

Jarrett Payton, 19. "From the day in February when my dad told the world about his liver disease, the outpouring of love, support and prayers from around the world astounded even him."

Jarrett Payton probably didn't realize he himself was astounding the media by showing up to thank people only five hours after his father's death. Brittney Payton, only 14, accepted the ARETE courage award for her dad only 10 days before he died.

"My father would like me to thank you for all the cards and the prayers," she said. "He is very excited about this award and is sorry that he's not able to be here to accept it in person. One of the downfalls of his illness is that he's very weak and tired. But his heart and soul are with you."

"We're still the same people we always were," Connie Payton once said. "People are surprised when they find we're so down to earth, but we're from the South and we only know one way to behave.

"People say, 'You're married to *him*!' And all I can think is, 'It's no big deal.' It's like my father said, 'He's lucky to be married to *you*.' "

Payton's teammates held him in as much awe as fans did. When the Bears planned a three-minute ceremony in 1984 after he broke Jim Brown's rushing record, Payton refused. "I'm not too excited about stopping the game for any length of time or making a ceremony," he said.

Jay Hilgenberg, one of the league's best centers throughout the '80s, remembers going to Pro Bowls with Payton. "I remember thinking how special that was," said Hilgenberg. "Here I am on the same team as Walter Payton in a Pro Bowl. And how he would treat me like a close teammate in front of all the NFL stars made me feel good. He was an incredible guy."

> ## "He couldn't just walk up and say, 'Hi, I'm Walter Payton.' He had to pick you up off the ground and almost break your ribs."
>
> — Bears teammate Gary Fencik

Payton didn't have to meet a player, or be a teammate, to create the same effect. Jerry Azumah, a fifth-round draft choice of the Bears this year, never met Payton but proudly displays a letter he received from him shortly after the draft.

"It was basically just congratulating me," said Azumah. "I was really pleased that he wrote me a letter and I have it hanging in my house. That was really nice."

Payton was not always nice. As a practical joker, humor is in the eye of the jokester.

"One time, our center, Dan Neal, was lying on a training table," Payton once revealed. "We had just come out with electrotherapy. He was all wired up, and I turned the juice as high as it could go. All his muscles were contracting."

Teammates never had to wonder who was behind the pranks. Did you ever hear the sound of an M-80 firecracker going off inside a racquetball court?

"He was always snapping towels and lighting cherry bombs," said quarterback Bob Avellini. "In a meeting when everybody is half asleep, he would give out an inhuman scream just for the hell of it."

Payton was the only suspect when the film projector mysteriously stopped in the middle of a meeting. If there was a funny smell, you could guess Payton had painted the projector light bulb with white-out. When a player found his shoestrings cut up the tongue of his cleats, he didn't have to look far for blame. Payton's aim with wadded-up tape or dirty socks was uncanny. Trainers have something called artificial fat tissue, which they use for padding linemen's

Payton was always as much of a crowd-pleaser off the field as he was on it, whether he was taking time out to spend with fans (left) or going up against New York Knicks center Patrick Ewing at a charity event in Chicago.

The Softer Side of Sweetness

hands. It looks like cheese, but it doesn't taste like cheese, according to players who have found it in their sandwiches. Paraffin wax is another training supply that can make a donut look but not taste glazed.

"If a car backfires, everybody blames me," Payton said. "I was in an assistant coach's office one day, and all of a sudden—boom!—a firecracker went off in the locker room. Everybody's running around screaming, 'Walter, where are you!' And I said, 'Coach, I've been sitting here with you, and you know it wasn't me. But I'm going to get blamed for this.'" Notice, Payton didn't deny it. He admitted to some knowledge of delayed fuses.

The hyper Payton needed to be doing something every minute. The day after he set the NFL rushing record of 275 yards in one game, he was busy running scout plays to get the Bears' defense ready for Detroit. "We tried to get him to rest, but he would pout because he wouldn't have anything to do during the defensive drills," said coach Jack Pardee.

During lunch break, he would commandeer the office switchboard from the receptionist and answer the phones.

Teammates loved the fact that Payton was the Bears' cutup off the field, yet no one was more serious about winning on the field.

"He had that high squeaky voice and nobody knew whether you were talking to a guy or a girl anyway," said coach Mike Ditka. "He'd really put you on. He used to get on the phone with me. I didn't know it was him."

Off the field, he had to work at being serious. He once interrupted a somber warning against drugs by an NFL security officer by sprinkling sugar in his mustache and yelling: "Ain't no cocaine on this team." On the field, he was dead serious, except for the times he would

"How he would treat me like a close teammate in front of all the NFL stars at the Pro Bowl made me feel good. He was an incredible guy."

— Bears teammate Jay Hilgenberg

untie an official's shoelace when he would spot the ball. Payton always tried to inch the ball ahead a bit and estimated he added 100 yards to his total that way. Whenever the referee would catch him and move the ball back, Payton would complain: "How do you expect me to catch Jim Brown that way?"

After fullback Matt Suhey fumbled once, Payton walked off the field with him and asked: "You ever have a paper route? You can always get a paper route, because you do that again and you won't be playing football for long."

The Bears could have charged admission to watch Payton practice. The repetition of football practice can bore the observer and mesmerize even the players, but not when Payton was around. During

considerable lag times, he would play catch with anyone he could find for as long as anyone dared.

"He threw more passes than the quarterbacks," said Fencik. "My lasting memory will be of going out and seeing Walter in a state of perpetual motion. I think it reflects in a real, positive way how much he really loved playing football."

One day, when practice was over and players and coaches were wearily walking toward the locker room, Payton sneaked up behind 6-foot-5 assistant coach Brad Ecklund, put his hands on his shoulders, and suddenly leaped-frogged over his head, scaring Ecklund out of his wits.

Payton explained that he laughed and joked while he could. "Life is so short, you

better enjoy it while you can," he said. "When you're a young kid, growing up seems like it takes a long time. But then you go off to first grade and realize how short it was."

Payton's mother, Mrs. Alyne Payton, didn't allow Walter to play football until he was a junior in high school. She remembers him as "sweet" long before football gave him the famous nickname. "When he was five and I was sick in bed, he brought me my pills," said Mrs. Payton.

Sister Pam recalled a slightly different version: "Not always the right pills. Sometimes he'd hide the right ones."

"Of course, they were full of mischief," agreed Mrs. Payton, including older brother Eddie. "Like when I was scared at nights and would crawl into their room," said Pam.

The Softer Side of Sweetness

"They'd have sheets tied to a rope outside their window and they'd pull them up and I'd think it was a ghost."

Added Mrs. Payton: "And the times they put a pail of water over the door when they knew you'd come in."

Concluded Pam: "Did they ever do anything nice? I can't recall."

Still, Payton's mother always believed there was more than football in Walter's future. "I always thought he would turn out to be a preacher," she said in 1977. "I still think he'll be a preacher. He's very serious, very religious. And he's only going to play three more years. At least, that's what he told me—if he's lucky to play that much. I don't want him to play any more than that."

Walter's father, Peter, and his mother worked at the Pioneer Recovery Co., makers of parachutes, in Columbia, Miss. Before the final game of the 1978 season, Payton's father died unexpectedly of a subdural hematoma, a blood clot in his brain. Payton quietly attended the funeral and returned to play in the last game, scoring on a 44-yard touchdown in the first three minutes.

The nickname Sweetness described his moves. Its origin moves Payton to more kidding around.

"I got it from the girls at Jackson State," he said.

Really?

"No, I really got it from the men," he said in a falsetto voice.

Really?

"No, I really got it from the other players at the College All-Star game."

Payton touched people in more subtle and profound ways than bear hugs or pranks. Mike Hartenstine, drafted in the second round in 1975, played his first 12 years with him. Their birthdays are two days apart and their

sons were born a month apart. Hartenstine seldom spoke much. "We went through a whole lot together early in our careers," said Hartenstine. "The thing I'll miss is the smile and the hug. He was like a brother to me. You could just feel the love there."

In the first three days after his death, the Bears' Web site received 1,002,782 hits from 54 countries to view the Payton tribute. Of those, 3,376 posted messages.

Payton once said: "People see what they want to see. They look at me and say, 'He's a black man. He's a football player. He's a running back. He's a Chicago Bear.' But I'm more than all that. I'm a father. I'm a husband. I'm a citizen. I'm a person who is willing to give his all. That's how I want to be remembered."

He was also a race car driver, professional and amateur, a restaurant owner and an entrepreneur. As part of his Bear

Payton and Ditka were recently reunited when the coach brought his New Orleans Saints to Soldier Field.

contracts negotiated by his former advisor Bud Holmes, Payton invested in forest land and nursing homes. He leased heavy equipment and made up to $1 million a year giving motivational speeches. With advisor Ginny Quirk, he turned Walter Payton Inc. into a full-time job of managing his money and appearances.

When Pete Rozelle was NFL commissioner, he came as close as a commissioner can come to promising Payton an expansion franchise. But labor problems and Rozelle's retirement forced Payton to join the rest of the crowd. He was in the picture for an expansion team in St. Louis before the league went to Jacksonville and Carolina. His latest foray into football was as an investor in the Arena League.

Since his retirement, he had been sitting on the Bears board of directors, although it seems folly to mention Payton and sitting in

the same sentence. He never pretended to be a perfect person or a perfect football player, although he came as close to the latter as anybody who ever tried. "He was the greatest Bear of all," said Ditka, a Hall-of-Famer himself.

The startling numbers in the record books only start to measure the greatness. Payton worked harder than anybody else to bridge the gaps between offense and defense, between black and white, between star and newcomer.

"He was the one guy who really pulled that team together in the '80s when it could have come apart," Ditka said. "We were kind of in factions on offense and defense and he really worked hard at pulling it together. He got each side to respect each other and we finally became a football team instead of an offense and a defense."

To most of the defensive players, Payton was the one and only offensive player who earned their total respect. "He's the first running back I ever saw who could have played defense," said Singletary.

Struck down by cancer at age 45, Payton found out about the disease last spring and refused to let the public know, just as he hated to reveal football injuries. Like Brian Piccolo, who had Gale Sayers, Payton had Matt Suhey with him every step of the way.

"The loyal, devoted, self-sacrificing friend," said Bears chairman emeritus Ed McCaskey. "The same thing happened here."

Friends said he never complained or lost his resolve or his sense of humor, sticking steadfastly to a lesson learned early from football: "Never die easy." In the end, he was with his wife and his son and his daughter, his mother, brother and sister, and he was at peace at last, said Singletary.

"I would think people will remember him as a guy who knew how to laugh, who loved to have fun," said Singletary. "A guy who was down to earth, a real person, the superstar who was touchable." **34**

"The thing I'll miss is the smile and the hug. He was like a brother to me. You could just feel the love there."

—Bears teammate Mike Hartenstine

Don Pierson is the pro football writer for the Chicago Tribune, covering the Bears from 1970-87 and the NFL at large since 1987.

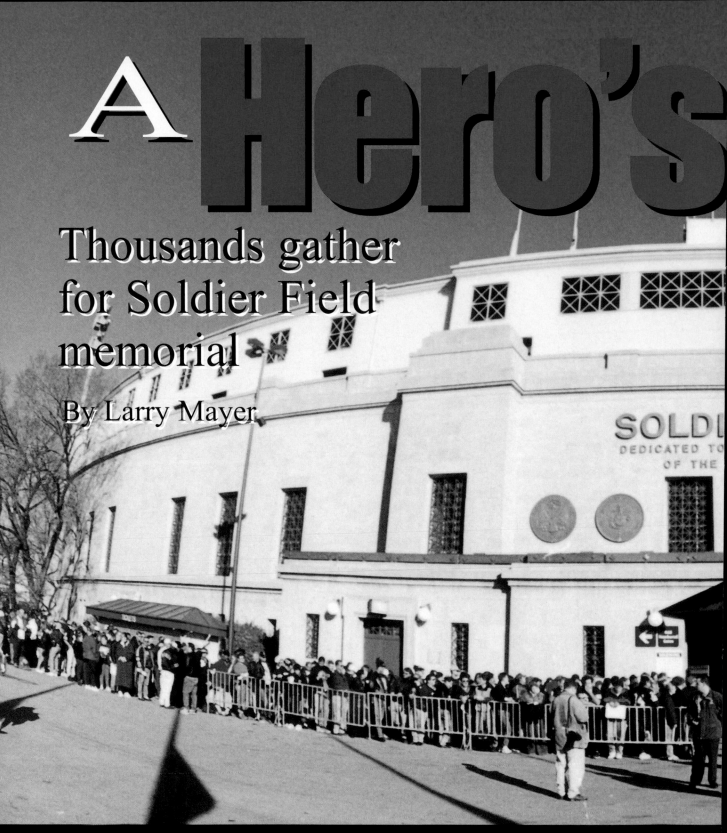

A Hero's

Thousands gather for Soldier Field memorial

By Larry Mayer

BEFORE THE GLORY YEARS of the mid-'80s, the incomparable Walter Payton was the only reason thousands of Chicago Bears fans spent autumn afternoons at Soldier Field.

History repeated itself Nov. 6 at the venerable stadium on Chicago's lakefront. Only this time, the No. 34 jerseys sprinkled throughout the crowd cloaked heavy hearts and were spotted with tears of sorrow.

In an unprecedented display of love and devotion, about 20,000 fans paid tribute to the life and legacy of the Hall-of-Fame running back who died Nov. 1 of bile duct cancer at age 45.

In attendance at the emotional 90-minute memorial service were Payton's family, 30 former Bears—many of whom were his teammates on the 1985 Super Bowl championship team—and every member of the current team and coaching staff. Also present were Bears owners Ed and Virginia McCaskcy and dignitaries such as Rev. Jesse L. Jackson and NFL commissioner Paul Tagliabue.

Flags bearing Payton's famous uniform

Farewell

number flew at half-staff; the 30-yard line was repainted as the recognizable "34," and a temporary Jumbotron scoreboard suspended by a crane beyond the north end zone showed highlights of his life set to music. The Sweet Holy Spirit Full Gospel Choir also provided inspirational musical interludes. The

program was emceed by former teammates and local sportscasters Mike Adamle and Dan Jiggetts along with sportscaster Tim Weigel.

One of the most beloved athletes of all time, Payton broke Jim Brown's career rushing record in 1984 and still holds the mark 15 years later with 16,726 yards. But the man they called

"Sweetness" was even more admired as a human being. Off the field, Payton's generosity and charisma fueled his status as a genuine hero who was idolized by countless admirers. After retiring from football, he coached high school basketball, read to children in

A Hero's Farewell

a literacy program, and anonymously donated thousands of dollars to charity.

"He just had a wonderful zest for life, and that's something that's unusual in people of his stature," said Jiggetts. "Most people of his stature who have achieved what he achieved in life really don't want to be

"I never met him, but I felt like he was a good friend," said fan Bill Mercer, 31, clad in a Payton jersey and sitting in the first row at midfield. "What he did off the field speaks volumes. That's even better than what he did on the field. I grew up with him. He reminds me of being a kid, and I just had to be here."

McMullen. "The things that he did in his private life, people are starting to recognize that. It just magnifies what he was on the field, and that's why I wanted my son to be here to see it.

"He meant a great deal to me as a person and as an athlete and as a role model because he was a role model. He accepted it. You never saw Walter with an entourage, you never heard about Walter getting into any problems. I wanted to come here and pay my respects and bring my son."

The elder McMullen wouldn't be surprised if Alexander one day trades the Elmo doll he was clutching for a football.

"Even though he's got Elmo in his hands, he's going to be the next Walter Payton as far as I'm concerned," said McMullen.

Signs scattered throughout the crowd included messages such as "Thank you for the memories," "We'll miss you Walter," and "Life is a little less sweet."

"Everybody ran around the front yard and yelled out Walter's name, and you jumped over your friend onto the couch head-

bothered with the general public. He was the exact opposite, and from the common guy on the street to heads of state to kings and queens, Walter was just that—Walter Payton."

"He was in many ways what we don't expect a superstar to be—open, accessible, genuine, down to earth, a unifier and a binder, never divisive," Tagliabue said.

Listening to the recollections of those who knew him best and loved him most created a somber yet celebratory mood at the memorial service.

Sanford McMullen, 41, was capturing the ceremony on videotape while holding his 2-year-old son, Alexander. "He was a great person outside of being a great athlete," said first," recalled fan Dave Schwieder, 32. "Everything Walter did, you wanted to do. It wasn't convenient to get down here, I just felt I had to do it. I loved the man."

It was fitting the tribute was held at Soldier Field, a place where Payton delighted Bears fans from 1975-87.

"I've got a little girl who's 4 years old," said former teammate Dan Hampton, his voice cracking. "Ten years from now when she asks me about the Chicago Bears, I'll tell her about a championship and I'll tell her about great teams, and great teammates and great coaches, and how great it was to be a part of it. But the first thing I'll tell her about is Walter Payton."

Before the service officially started, fans were treated to a montage of video highlights. One NFL Films clip described Payton as "a back with the toughness of a Tonka Toy and the quickness of a cat."

The crowd's favorite highlight package was similar to the one televised on "The NFL Today." It featured Payton's

Below, current Chicago Bears place flowers at the base of a famous photograph, while NFL Commissioner Paul Tagliabue (far left) and Rev. Jesse L. Jackson (above) speak to nearly 20,000 attendees at Soldier Field.

most remarkable runs in slow motion set to the words and music of the song "Nobody Does It Better."

"I remember when I was growing up in Pennsylvania in 1977," said former Bears tackle Jim Covert, a Payton teammate. "I watched the video that you all watched here where it says 'Nobody Does It Better.' And nobody ever did it better than Walter Payton. Nobody."

The musical tributes were as powerful as one of Payton's patented stiff-arms. That's because Sweetness was simultaneously as fluid as a saxophone riff and as relentless as a drum solo. He was never the biggest or fastest running back in the league, but his sheer will to achieve could move mountains, not to mention overmatched linebackers. He came, he saw, he high-stepped. His quickness and elusiveness were legendary, but he seemed to take the most pride in running over and through defenders.

The NFL's all-time leading rusher initiated many of the violent collisions, dishing out punishment most running backs only absorb. Then he sprang to his feet and helped befuddled opponents off the ground with a playful pat on the behind. He fought for every extra yard and never ran out of bounds. He was respected by fans, teammates and opponents alike. He was told the crowd. "On this Soldier Field and between these goal posts and on dozens more, he was, as Mike Ditka said, a football warrior and a gladiator. He never gave up. He was seemingly indestructible, and in the eyes of many, he was the greatest football player of all time."

"Long before their was a Super Bowl title in Chicago, Walter Payton taught us what it was like to be a champion," said Cook County Board President John Stroger.

The memorial service opened with the introduction of the former Bears. Then the appearance of the current team elicited chants of "Beat the Pack, Beat the Pack." The '99 Bears later left the ceremony early to travel to Green Bay for a game the following day against the rival Packers. Several Bears have dedicated the remainder of the season to Payton's memory.

"Speaking for the players in our locker room," defensive tackle Jim Flanigan told the crowd, "we will do our best to uphold Walter's legacy and to honor his memory in our fight, our pride and our intensity."

"For the rest of this season, I'll play for Walter and his family and his ex-teammates," added tackle James "Big Cat" Williams. "I'll keep them all

simply the heart and soul of the Bears both on and off the field.

Yet while Payton's incredible drive helped him hurdle every obstacle on the football field, he was unable to win the battle for his life. It's a cruel irony that the same indestructible body that enabled him to miss only one game in 13 NFL seasons was ravaged with a fatal disease. Payton died at his South Barrington home of cancer that was a complication of primary sclerosing cholangitis, a rare liver disease he had suffered from since last fall.

"He was a warrior, a neighbor and a friend," Tagliabue

A Hero's Farewell

Bears won the Super Bowl.

"I was prancing over to the practice field, so proud to be with all these great legends on a wonderful warm afternoon in sunny Hawaii," recalled Duerson. "After about three minutes it started getting awfully warm. Walter had put some unscented liquid heat in my jock. It was a very hot afternoon in warm, sunny Hawaii."

Even in death, Payton continued to help the less fortunate.

In lieu of flowers or donations, his family asked fans to bring unwrapped toys to the event to assist the Walter Payton Foundation's "Wishes to Santa Program." The toys will be distributed to the Department of Children and Family Services for the holiday season and given to 50,000 wards of the state.

In addition, volunteers from the Illinois Secretary of State's office passed out organ donor cards to fans entering the stadium. After Payton announced in February that he was suffering from a rare liver disease and needed a transplant to survive, much attention was focused on the state's organ donor program.

in my heart and in my head."

Williams joked about the time he and Payton were making an appearance together in a shopping mall and the legendary running back entered a jewelry store and tried to sell wedding bands to two customers. "He's probably one of the greatest men I've ever met, not because of what he did on the field, but how special he made you feel off the field," said Williams.

Fans shed tears but also shared in the laughter at the recollections of Payton's legendary pranks. He routinely set off cherry bombs in team dormitories during training camp and pulled other practical jokes to keep his teammates loose. Safety Dave Duerson remembered trying to enjoy his first practice with the NFC Pro Bowl squad in Hawaii a few days after the

Payton's family listens to the poignant remarks at the memorial service.

When Payton's cancer was discovered in May, it precluded him from receiving a life-saving transplant.

Duerson displayed his signed organ donor card and encouraged others to join him. "You too can make a difference," he said. "You talk about a celebration of life, you have an opportunity to give the gift of life."

The service concluded with words from Payton's son, Jarrett; his wife, Connie, and his brother, Eddie. Also in attendance were Payton's daughter, Brittney, his mother, Alyne, and his sister, Pam. His father, Peter, died in 1978.

"We're so thankful for all the support we've had from all the people in Chicago," said Jarrett, an 18-year-old freshman running back at the University of Miami.

"I thank everybody in Chicago for caring and loving Walter as much as the kids and I do," added Connie.

A final musical tribute left few dry eyes. Set to the Sarah McLachlan song, "I Will Remember You," it featured Payton

A Hero's Farewell

SOLDIER FIELD
DEDICATED TO THE MEN AND WOMEN
OF THE ARMED SERVICES

holding both of his children when they were toddlers, running the famous hill he conditioned on and throwing out the first ball at a Cubs game.

Though his family wept at the conclusion of the ceremony, the tremendous composure they displayed throughout the yearlong ordeal is proof that Payton's legacy will live on long after his football records are shattered.

"He was a superb athlete but he also was a man of great dignity," said Rev. Jackson. "He fought the good fight, he kept the faith and he finished the journey. His light went out too quickly. We will never forget the brilliance of his glow." **34**

Larry Mayer is the Managing Editor of the Chicago Bear Report.

Tears flowed abundantly at the memorial service. Clockwise from top left, owner Virginia McCaskey; wife Connie Payton; one of the thousands of Soldier Field fans, and brother Eddie Payton show their respects.

WALTER, "THANKS FOR BEING THERE"

In His Own Words

"To some of you, I don't look healthy. I still am. Most of you guys I can still take!"

— Feb. 2, 1999

"The people that really care about me, if you could continue to pray. And to those who want to say what they say, God be with you also."

— Feb. 2, 1999

"I was standing up in the house and I'm putting on my clothes and my clothes didn't fit and my chest and stomach started to hurt and I just felt sorry for myself and broke down in tears because of the way I looked. You waste too much time doing that."

— Feb. 5, 1999

"I'm not a good role model. I'm just Walter Payton. If kids see some good in me they can utilize and emulate and make their lives better, so well and so good. But they have to realize I'm human just like anybody else. I'm capable of making mistakes. I'm capable of making the wrong decision. They should realize that. Nobody's perfect. Please don't put that on me, because I'm not perfect."

— On his influence

"It's just like football. You never know when or what your last play is going to be. You just play it and play it because you love it. Same way with life. You live life because you love it. If you can't love it, you just give up hope."

— Feb. 5, 1999

"I don't perceive myself as being better than anyone. I shovel my driveway. I go to the grocery store. I pump my own gas. Some athletes don't do that."

— During a 1993 interview

"I used to spike it or give it to my offensive linemen (to spike). Now, I just drop it and get ready for the next series. I think that's more professional than putting on a show. Most of the time when you put on a show, it's simply to excite the crowd and to kind of taunt the other team. But a lot of times, that gives them more incentive to come back and not let you get it in there again."

- On end zone celebrations, 1987

"My 11,000-yard checkup."

- After surgery on both knees after the 1983 season

"Once my career is over, whatever happens, it's God's will. I have no control over it. As far as anyone coming along and breaking that record, I have no quarrels about it. Just as long as it's my son."

- Before breaking Jim Brown's career rushing record in 1984

"I want to set the record so high that the next person who tries for it, it's going to bust his heart."

- Before setting the all-time rushing record

"It's not a matter of pride, it's a matter of survival. Because if you let those guys beat up on you, you won't be in there too long. So what you have to do instead of being on offense, you have to take the defensive approach sometimes."

- On delivering blows to tacklers

"I look at tape of myself, not to see what I did on a play, but what I could have done to make it better. There are too many has-beens who got that way by looking back and getting satisfied."

- From a 1981 interview

"I'm not a star. People who don't know much about football say I'm a star. It's important to me to just be one with my teammates."

- During the 1977 season, his best statistically

Payton's **Place**

Payton's Place

Payton's
Place

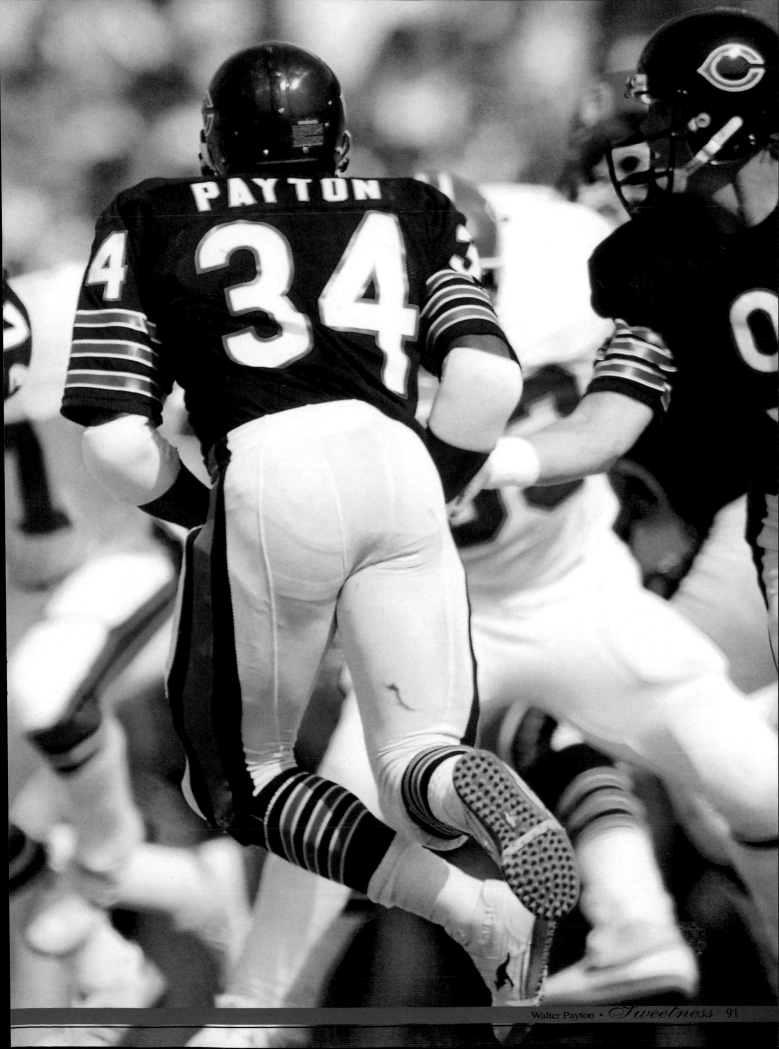

Payton's
Place